CW00433156

'T is The Irish Way

Margot Bish

'T is The Irish Way

By

Margot Bish

Other titles by Margot Bish

How Could I Forget? Short story for 3-5 yr olds

The Long Day Out   Short story for 3-5 yr olds

The Perfect Home   Short story for 3-5 yr olds

Through The Storm   (for 8-12 year olds)

A Difficult Age   (for teenagers and adults)

A Moment In Time   for adults

Chapter 1 :   The Beginning

It all started with a decision.

It was high time I learned to ride a horse.

After all, being something over fifty, I was in " now or never" territory. Browsing blearily through websites it occurred to me that I could combine this with my craving to further explore either Ireland or Scotland – both visited once, my memories treasured. I had another idea. Maybe I could also combine it with my desire to go white water rafting. After further browsing, I realised this was maybe a step too far and deleted the white water rafting – hey, I'll do that next year. Excitedly, I found a stable on Ireland's west coast which didn't actually exclude adults or individuals (as opposed to groups) and contacted them. Could they teach a single adult rider aged over 50, complete novice at the beginning of March? Yes they could. Where could I stay? To be sure, there's a B&B just down the road we have an arrangement with. I could fly over and they would collect me if I liked from the airport. Never one to make things easy, I declined the offer, explaining that I did not get along with airports and aeroplanes and I would, instead have an adventure on the trains and ferries with my trusty bicycle. It would take a great deal longer but meant I would see more of Ireland as I whizzed across from Dublin to Sligo by superfast, super comfortable train and then cycled 20 miles up the coast.

Does anyone else hate booking things via the internet as I do? The options creating stresses and hair tearing are infinite. I spent hours getting highly frustrated at ferries that didn't tell me I couldn't take a bicycle until 5 minutes into the booking, OK, delete Liverpool and Fishguard. Trains from Cork to Sligo took over a day so narrowed things down to "from somewhere" to Dublin. I did consider cycling from Cork when I saw the train journey time from Redditch, where I live, to Holyhead and that my ferry would leave at 2am.Way after my bedtime. Every section of the journey was about 3 hours so nowhere would I get a good sleep. Well, hey, I could do that 8 years ago. Time to see what I could still do. Snooze at home noon to 4pm, eat, catnap through journey, one hour at a time and sleep again 28 hours later – sure - no problem.

I need to tell you now that I am a serious technophobe. I can operate a computer, but have no broadband at home and mobile phones are inventions of the devil designed to gobble up the world's electricity and cause extreme flooding, droughts, wildfires and deserts, so I refuse to have one. I therefore have to use the library for online booking and cannot do the password thing when they then want to send it to my phone......which is 2 miles away, at home and doesn't do texts anyway. What should I book first? So many choices - two trains, no make that three, a ferry and two bed and breakfasts so not many things to go wrong. I thought I would do the ferry first as this had the least flexibility. I smiled happily and quietly hopped up and down triumphantly in my seat as it allowed me to book for one adult with a bicycle, and the library printer sprang into action, printing off far too many bits of booking information on reams of paper for my planet loving soul.....and then the blow fell. It wanted a mobile phone number to alert me to ferry cancellations! What to do? Whatever number I gave, someone else would know the ferry was cancelled but they wouldn't be able to tell me. I considered adding an unsuspecting friend's number (done before and causing said friend to wonder why Argos were telling him there was an item ready for collection at their Redditch branch. I didn't get home to explain this to him via my landline until four hours later. Fortunately, being on holiday in Devon at the time he hadn't followed the message up), but decided my Mum's number would be better. Really, it would make no difference as I would be en route on the train and would simply find out on arrival at Holyhead where I would patiently wait for the next ferry to sail. Probably, travelling in oblivious anticipation was better than miserably knowing I would be arriving four hours too early before I even got there. So, ferry booked, I moved onto the Irish train, a little frustrating that while dithering on the ferry booking, all the cheapest outward rail tickets seemed to have gone, but it was only 4 euros extra and the journey all across Ireland from east coast to west cost only 20 euros even then, whereas the titchy off peak journey to Holyhead was more than double. The bicycle booking was easy – big box on the screen to tick and no money to pay – well done Ireland, oh and hey, only one website to book through, too. I didn't have a choice of twenty five rail ticket companies all selling me the same tickets in twenty five different round about ways with different add ons for postage or management charges. Terrific. I was only a little nervous that technophobe Bish would have to use a ticket machine in Dublin to access her tickets and remember to take the booking ref number with me, correctly written. Ooh er. So there I am. well psyched up and on a roll, ready to tackle the UK system. I chose the Welsh rail site as it was their train and I had a bicycle space to reserve. Got through to the paying page and hadn't found a cycle reservation space. I found some splurge. "If you wish to book a bicycle, ring this number, there is no guarantee on ticket booking that a bicycle reservation can be made." Why is this so difficult in the UK? Every rail company seems to have a different policy aimed to make cyclists give up and take the car. OK. So do I now race home and do the train and then race back to book the guest houses or do I take a chance? Ah. The Monopoly question. I book the guest house in Sligo and e-mail The Donegal Stables to say, please provisionally book me, I just have to check the train works. Then I race for home, worried that the last bicycle space will be reserved while I am racing home. I am in luck. A nice lady books me on a different, faster train with less waiting time than I had dared risk at Crewe. "Do you want your tickets sent to you?" she asks.

"Yes please", I reply (yippee, no ticket machine to negotiate with). "OK", she says, after a pause. "Your tickets are sent second class at a cost of £1 but you will have to collect your bicycle reservation tickets from the ticket machine at Redditch station. Can I help you with anything else?" I have just paid an extra pound for the sending of the tickets which I might as well have collected from the machine with the bike tickets. I decide it's not the lady's fault so do not rant and rave down the line or ask her to come and do the ticket machine thing for me and drop them down the road. It will be good practice for Ireland, I tell myself as I write down the very long reference number. The next day, I head back to the library to book the stables and their B&B and ask if I can pay by cash on arrival. I wait around but get no reply. The English pound is on a dive as everyone outside England steadily loses confidence in our politicians. I decide to go and get the money anyway.

Who knows, I might make a profit if the nose dive continues. When I get back to the library, I discover a request to pay by credit card or paypal. (Bother, my credit card has just been destroyed as the company got fed up with me not using it and sulkily said they wouldn't let me have it anymore. Just typical that a week later I find I could have borrowed some money from them after all). Paypal and my bank cheerfully add on as many transaction charges as they can think of and typically use a much higher rate of euros to pounds than my cash transaction. Luckily, I am now on an excited high as I tick everything off – trains, ferry, more trains, two b&bs and the stables. I'M SORTED. Now – how do I cycle from Sligo to where I want to go? Along the coast or over the hills? I see there is a waterfall not far from the direct route. I LOVE waterfalls. So much uncontrollable power and exuberance. Can I add this in? We-ell, yes but it makes it 26 miles, not 20. I check the times of trains and decide it would be no fun as I would be feeling the pressure of time. If I cycle along the coast, though on my exploring days, then I could see the waterfalls – yes, there are TWO – on the way back to Sligo and come through the mountains (Wow). My dream is coming together, and I feel excited. I use Google maps to check the gradients and views and see that there are views of the sea from the hilltops and actually, I can't see much sea from the coastal route unless I go off route and cycle up dead end lanes. I always find this dispiriting as retracing my steps, or in this case cycle tracks, seems a waste of exploring time. Somewhere along the way, I realise that the Irish first language is Gaelic and not English, as I had originally thought – how amazingly bilingual nearly all the Irish are. I always think it is rude not to attempt to speak a country's local language so I look for a Gaelic- English dictionary. The dictionary I discover in the library is in fact more of a phrase book but the phrases are fascinating. It seems that the Irish live a very dramatic life. Phrases such as "Lauren always welcomes the stranger to her door." "Shamus is the father of many sons." "His mood was as black as the storm" dominated and nowhere could I find, "Could you direct me to Sligo, please,"

"How much are these postcards?" or "I would like to order a meal, please". I could have discoursed for hours about boats, flowers, wars and sheep and the slaying of hundreds. Discussions on the types of rain, marshland and wind strengths would have been easy to partake in but it took days to assemble the sentence "I have lost my way, could you show me where I am on this map, please?" I was also amused to find that Right and Left had the same words as east and west (or was it north and south) anyway it would make directions quite misleading at times. I decided that whatever happened, I must not get lost, but then could not find a large scale map of light enough weight to carry on a bicycle. I had a bright idea. Memorise the route using Google maps and draw pictures of all the important turnings because I noticed the Irish do not like spoiling their amazingly beautiful scenery by erecting sign posts on the more scenic routes. Luckily, once in the uplands, for 10 miles I would just have to keep the mountain escarpment on my right, and if I missed my turn, would eventually run out of road at a t-junction –

only 5 miles beyond the turning I should have taken! I buy a smaller scale map as a backup, more suitable for main road travel.

Chapter 2: The Journey

So. Here we are at Birmingham New Street railway station. Gales have roared across the Irish Sea and the UK for the last four days, but the ferry company has not yet cancelled my ferry. Indeed, the weather forecasters are promising me a lull of 24 hours before the next set of 50mph winds arrive, and I'm really enjoying the luck of my great grandfather's Irish blood. The winds have been consistently from the West. Why is this important? You ask. Ah haaaa. The ferry will be going straight into the waves and not rolling across them thus reducing sea-sickness – thank goodness. I can't help feeling smug because, with 15 minutes to go, my train is still listed as "on time". I have been feeling sorry for the Wolverhampton people whose train is delayed due to "vehicle hitting bridge" – no time is given for that train's arrival so I guess they will be joining us on our train, which also stops there. I try not to feel too smug as I superstitiously think smugness, a little like pride comes before a fall. …….and

I am proved right as, two minutes later, our train is also delayed due to vehicle hitting bridge, but it's OK as the delay is only two minutes and I have ten minutes in hand. Of course, smug spotting fate knows this and two minutes later, adds on another two minutes and then corrects this to five.

Should I get the train that goes via Shrewsbury instead? It's much slower, but no changes. I hesitantly wander up to a knowledgeable looking station man in his super orange vis-vest and consult. He consults his little magic box which tells me to hold my nerve. "Are you taking the bike?" he asks. I nod. "OK, well go to that end of the platform", he indicates with a nod. "And I'll be there to help you on board." What a nice man, I think as I amble up the platform, noticing that the delay time has now reduced and the train is now due in one minute. Just as I get as far away from the lift as possible in order to be ckose to the bicycle carriage, there is an announcement."PLATFORM CHANGE THE TRAIN TO CREWE IS NOW ARRIVING AT PLATFORM 8". We are on platform 5. It is quite exciting dancing through the hoards aiming for the escalator while I struggle to dash the other way towards the lift without smacking too many passengers in the shins with my pedals. I share the lift with a frazzled lady and her very large suitcase muttering dire curses against all last minute train change announcers if she misses the train. I just mutter hurry up mantras at the slow moving lift. The door pings open to a breezy announcement of "Doors opening" and I dash out. Nearly everyone is on board, but which way to the bicycle carriage? With a mental toss of a coin I head to the left. A station man appears. "Are you on this train?" he asks. I resist the urge to say no, I want to be on it but I am presently on the platform and say "Yes". "This way," he says as we run along the platform – now deserted. I am impressed with his turn of speed but manage to keep up. The train driver is not impressed. He's already late and here is some crazy overloaded cyclist making him later. "Where to?" he grunts. "Crewe", we reply in unison. He nods grudgingly. I guess this is not so bad as it his last stop so won't cause further delays unloading. I get on board quite neatly with rucksack and all bicycle attachments still living up to their description – attached and find myself in a sort of coffin space – a little unnerving. Investigation reveals some straps for tying bicycles and a big notice by the one sliding door which advises me to tell the train staff in carriage C I have a bicycle on board. I strap my bike in and issue it with instructions not to get pinched and not to fall over and exit via the sliding door, which has no access button on the carriage side of the door – ah ha, so this is why I must visit carriage C. Just a little annoying as my seat is in carriage F, carefully selected as being close to the bicycle carriage but hey, I'm fit, I can do this.

Carriage C is the home of the buffet and two cheerful ladies in uniform holding an animated conversation about fashion and film stars. I hover. "Can I help you luv? " The accent is Manchurian. I explain about the notice and my locked in bicycle. "Daphne will tell the conductor, won't you Daph?" she assures me. Daph nods. "I'll remind her," she adds. They resume their conversation with enthusiasm and I think that maybe I will try to find the conductor and tell him myself......just in case. The driver does his best to make up lost time as we click through the stations and arrives at Crewe only two minutes late, and the door to the bicycle compartment slides open like something in a James Bond or Star Trek movie with no apparent manual aid (Mind you, with Daph, the conductor AND the driver all made aware, I would have been surprised if the door had remained shut). We –my bike and I – alight smoothly, and also clamber onto our connection with ease. No sci-fi stuff here, which suits me fine. I am now quite expert at lifting my bike above my head to hook the wheel in a frame designed for six foot guys so long as the train is stationary. I flop into a seat and doze my way along the North Wales coast noting the stops where we used to scramble among castle ruins – Flint and Conwy and Caernavon or paddled off sandy beaches as children on days out, whilst living in Chester. I wonder, now if our imaginations got the clothes right as we played out battle scenes, never sure if the baddies were the Welsh or the English, my sister was born in Wales. I was born in England but learned to talk and walk amongst the Welsh and my childhood friends were all Welsh until moving back to Chester at the age of 3 so my loyalties were certainly mixed. Holyhead was a long time coming but the train was warm and a safe place to snooze. The Holyhead ferry terminal is under shelter but sparse. No seats you could stretch out in. I pass a man, head down on his walking frame and snoring, a couple asleep on each other's head and shoulders, and check my watch. One and a half hours to wait. The most comfortable place appears to be the floor, so I unpack a coat and towel, plump up my rucksack, set my alarm for 1 hour twenty, tuck myself in and sleep. I suppose most people travel by car but why, when we are supposed to be encouraging environmentally friendly travel is there nowhere to at least lay your head back and put your feet up? Luckily, I am still good at catnapping and wake feeling ready to go. The check-in opens surprisingly close to leaving time and no one seems to be in any hurry. Four guys in uniform loiter in a passageway as I pass through with my bike. I hesitate. Do they want to check my bits of paper? Or my rucksack? They nod at me but say nothing. I move on and arrive at a staircase, still pushing my bike. Up there? One of the men calls out to me. "Would you like me to put your bike down the chute?" "Um. Is that what I'm supposed to do?" I ask. He nods. "Well, yes please then…..thankyou" The lack of signposting is surprising. The next surprise is that foot passengers actually board a bus to get to the ferry and we are driven on to the lorry deck. I am amused to find I look like someone who knows what they are doing as several people ask me where the cabins are, how they get their suitcases back and where the cafes are. I have simply followed the guy in front of me who seems to know where he is going, and in fact he does as he selects a quiet settee on deck G at the bow end, starboard side, removes his shoes and lies down. Good idea I think and take the next settee – not quite as peaceful as I can hear the sound effects from the children's jungle room – why are these running at two in the morning? but two repetitions in, I sleep, a little amused by the captain apologising for the delay which he nearly allocated to technological problems but changed his mind and made it congestion in the port. Was that less worrying?

I wake to hear the jungle effects are still rotating. There is no breakfast being served – unbelievable with a half hour to landing time. I always travel with emergency rations so don't starve, eating a flapjack, nuts, an apple and a carton of orange juice, but I'm disappointed and can't believe that breakfast wouldn't have been a profitable meal to serve at 5am. The captain apologises that we are now even later due to strong headwinds. Time is getting tight for catching my train. I had allowed an hour to cover what should have been a ten minute ride but leaving Holyhead ten minutes late and arriving now 30 minutes late is a little stressful. We are recalled to the bus and I try not to watch the bus clock ticking round as the priority lorries unload ahead of us. I KNOW that watching the time will make no difference to whether I catch the train or not but still can't remove my gaze for more than 30 seconds at a time. At last we move. There is a short unguided tour of the ferry port and then more stairs to where the baggage and bicycles will appear. I gaze out of the door and realise it doesn't look like the Google map. Which way to the station? I now have twelve minutes to do the ten minute journey. A visvest man is hovering and this is where I blow it. "Could you tell me how to get to the station?" I ask him. "Which station?" he asks. I should have checked my ticket info paper, but in a state of suppressed panic, I don't. "I want to get to Sligo," I reply. "That'd be Herlihy," he says. I have no reason to dispute this. "Turn right out of here." He pauses thoughtfully. "There's a tunnel and you can't go through it, but, don't worry. You'll find a way round it," he comforts me with a cheerful smile, in true Irish fashion. "Then follow the signs to the city, cross the river and go straight on. You can't miss it".

I'm worried about the tunnel and the lorries roaring passed me are terrifying in the dawn light even though every driver has been wonderful and has given the crazy cyclist a very wide berth. I do find a way round the tunnel but am now not sure if I'm still on the right route. The Google map seemed to have simply shown me cycling happily along the river and I seem to be meandering around a large number of docks. I ask another man who also thinks Herlihy is the place to go. Across the river and straight on. I find the river and cross it but hit a T junction' How do I go straight on? I stop another man. "Oh. Up the Liffey", he points. "A long way. Go! Go! Go!!" He waves his arms wildly to urge me on my way. I pedal on, finding it difficult to look for sign posts and not wobble in what is probably rush hour traffic. There are also cyclists whizzing about, all knowing where they are going with me in the way. The time ticks by and I think, one minute to go. OK so I missed the train. Stop panicking. At this point, I think I will check my train ticket info and discover I'm headed for the wrong station. Its Connolly I want. A lady points back across the river "Across the river and straight on," she says I am now ready for the anticipated t junction, but see the railway way above my head and reckon if I just follow the line I'll get there. The Dubliners are marvellous people. Everyone I stopped and asked did their very best to give me clear instructions with concentration, a smile and goodwill. The last issuer of guidance points at a two storey grey building. "Over there. You see that grey building? That's it", he says with a note of triumph. Hooray, I've made it and if I have to buy new tickets for the next train, I don't care. I can see a station entrance but it's at the top of an escalator. No way is my overloaded bicycle getting up there. People must have suitcases, I reason. There has to be another way. I check out what turns out to be a tramway across Dublin. No, not that. Around the other end of the building I encounter some imposing stone lions and a covered alleyway. Within the alley, on my right, there are stone steps leading up to the station. But they look steep too. I turn away. There MUST BE A LIFT. A man stops me to ask where he can get his tickets from a machine. I suggest he tries up the steps and am amused again that people think I know where I'm going. There is a sign directing me to the lift. I look doubtfully at a sliding door which might be a lift but has no buttons so maybe it's just a security door for the adjoining restaurant. I walk on and reach the other end of the alley. No lift. I turn and find another lift directing sign pointing back the way I've come. I retrace my steps and, then again. No lift. It must be that metal door. There's a hole where the button should be. I hopefully push my fingers in but nothing happens, so I have to take the stairs. I achieve this without falling or dropping the bike and feel a buzz of success. The man is still puzzling over a ticket machine which I take as a bad omen but spread out my wrinkled ticket info paper, stretch my fingers and wiggle them in the time honoured psyche myself up to something difficult way and press buttons. To my amazement, a ticket drops into the tray and then one more – just two, but wow, all the info is there. For my English trains, I am juggling 9 pieces of card. In Ireland, just two tickets. I almost give a leap of delight for the simplicity and efficiency of the Irish system. Of course, I am still in uncertainty land as I have missed the train. I find some timetables. There is another train in one and a half hours but will I be allowed on it with my bicycle? In England there would be whistles, pursing of lips and head shaking. In Dublin, as I explain my getting lost and missing my train, the ticket office man gives me a sympathetic and cheerful smile and assures me I can take the next train, platform 4 at 12 o' clock no trouble. "Is it OK with my bike?" I ask. It will be no problem. I am fascinated by Connolly station which seems to have a tidal system – a slow moving wave of people heading trainwards followed by a rushing tidal wave of swirling crowds heading out into Dublin, then fifteen minutes of calm seas before the next tidal rush. It was difficult to not get swept away in the tide. I was also intrigued by the ticket barriers. Were the tickets bar coded or were people waving passes at the barrier? I study my ticket. Is there a right way up? I then realise, with my bicycle that

I have an excuse to bypass the machinery
(There's my technophobic persona showing
again) and go to the man at the barrier for
disabled people. I give him a grin and try to
show him my ticket. "Where to?" he asks.
"Sligo," I tell him confident in everything
except pronunciation. He shakes his head.
"Another hour", he says. I explain about
getting lost. Another shake of the head,
sympathetic this time. He isn't exactly
barring entry but I get the message. Why
waste an hour sitting on a platform when
you could be exploring our beautiful city?
He is right of course, but what about those
stairs and my bicycle? Well, I will just have
to figure it out. I wander out to the
escalator. Not that way, wander back in,
dodge a tidal wave and in the peaceful
aftermath see another lift sign. Right. I
reckon this is the glass top of the lift with
no button. Will it work? Too awful if I get
stuck. Tentatively, I push the "door open"
button. The door obediently slides open. I
enter, push the inside button. The door
shuts and the lift stays exactly where it is.
There are no other buttons to press except
the "open door" button". How

embarrassing. I'm standing going nowhere in a glass lift. No one seems to have noticed. Quickly I press the door open button and exit. It doesn't seem worth pretending I did it all on purpose because no one would believe me. A quick glance around. No one is laughing. Right, I will leave my bike chained to a map post and go down the escalator. At this moment, I spot another lift but find my nerve has failed in the matter of lift negotiation and ignore it.

Dublin is beautiful. I loved the River Liffey, swirling green and clean, and the set-back skyscrapers of glass and steel creating a freedom of space and light. I am delighted at the separation of vehicles, the tram streets and bicycle tracks which I had not spotted in panic mode. Yet another couple ask me how to find a particular theatre. I have to admit my lack of local knowledge. I find a museum to wander round and even work out my route back to the ferry port before heading back to the station with ten minutes to spare, gaining the approval and a big smile from the gate man who still doesn't check my ticket but directs me to platform 4 – do I really stand out from the crowd so that he remembered me out of all those thousands of people an hour later? I am impressed. It seems that Irish people use the trains to get to work in Dublin, but during the day they have few users which is a shame as they are fast, comfortable and inexpensive. The scenery is beautiful and I find my Gaelic would have been useless as the station announcements are in Gaelic and English and even knowing what was being said I can't pick out a single recognisable word – not even the station name. I am now relaxed having worked out that if I do not get lost again and average 12mph I will arrive exactly on time for my riding lesson . I should be able to do that. No one will be worried because I will be on time.

The weather is changeable. Sun at low level, snow on the tops of Dublin's mountains. Likely temperature betwen 8 deg C and 14 deg c depending on cloud cover and amount of wind chill. I start to plan what I should wear for maximum bicycle speed. Don't get me wrong, I'm no lycra queen looking for least wind friction, but I do cycle best when not too hot or freezing cold or soaking wet. The sun feels hot through the train window. I pull, from my rucksack, shorts and lightweight shirt, and then as the train heads into the hills and cloud forms, add a cagoule. The cloud thickens. We lose the sun and the scenery becomes quite dramatic with jutting cliffs under a black sky. I add waterproof trousers as the rain drives sideways obliterating the mountains and then also add my anorak to go under my cagoule. Hailstones replace the rain. I peer hopefully into my rucksack but, no, I haven't brought anything for hail. I eat a chocolate bar for comfort. The best I can do. Thankfully, as we descend the mountains, we leave the fearsome clouds with their hailstones behind and the sun reappears with its cheerful glow. With relief, I put the anorak and waterproof trousers away. The trees wave wildly in the gale force winds. Thoughtfully, I also put away the shorts. Tracksuit trousers will be fine. I pull a sweatshirt to the top. Just in case. I drink an orange juice to avoid dehydration.

I feel the adrenalin pump as we slow, and stop at Sligo station. I already have my bike out of its rack, sweatshirt now in the saddlebags and rucksack on my back. It has been hard to decide whether to load the saddlebags or my rucksack. Heavy saddlebags make it harder to lift the bike off the train but heavy rucksack means it will be harder to stand on the pedals for that one steep hill. I spread things around a bit, but keep most weight in the rucksack, intending to shift it when I am out of the station. In fact the adrenalin kick has me running down the station steps, swinging on to my saddle and whizzing northwards, hoping I am going the right way. After a while, I control the fight or flight instinct enough to check the map and memorise the next few turns, proud of myself for learning (eventually) from the Dublin experience.

The roads in Ireland are a dream for cyclists. In over a hundred miles of road, I encountered only one bumpy surface. There were wide areas between the tarmac edge and the white line marking the motorised vehicle lane on main roads so I felt safe, even looking at the scenery as I belted along, determined not to drop below 12mph even on the uphill gradients. The sun shone and shone and the strong winds were dispersed by good healthy hedgerows. My milometer clocked up the miles and right on cue, the five fork junction next to restaurant appeared. Knowing getting lost would completely destroy my rescue plan, I got out my junction drawings and checked. Yep. Second road from the left. This was the biggest hill but only one and a half miles long. It was easy, as the 40mph westerly wind pushed helpfully at my rucksack and I literally sailed up the narrow lane, ticking off the landmarks of farms, gates and bends and repeating the left, right, right, long distance, left mantra as I pedalled. I had googled that journey so many times that it flew by like a repetitive dream with me on a mega adrenalin high. The scenery was immense. The roads were all mine – just one car in 13 miles. My only hesitations were caused by the householders who had repainted their doors and windows a deep shiny blue, replacing the flaky light blue of times gone by when the google camera passed by. Luckily, they had retained the distinctive side gate to confirm my route, and then some overzealous gardeners had taken down their rhododendron hedge. Was this the correct left turn? I gazed uncertainly down the hill. Oh yes, there's the tree bisecting the barn hayloft window, I thought and whizzed onwards. Some of the Google building sites were now immense white painted mansions, whilst others had gone for timber frame and wide glass panels embracing the wild views. I wondered about the Irish economy. Were these the homes of invaders or the Irish, and how big was the gap between this show of wealth and the average worker? Did farming pay in this still green land with its history of famine and poverty? I hoped so. The fantastic smooth tarmac took me downhill, through a small town across the major road with its free flowing traffic - the reason why I had the uplands to myself – and onto a ribbon development road of shops, B&B's, and side streets of houses with glimpses of the sea. Almost there. Google had insisted that I must divert through a housing estate along quite a complicated route and refused to let me go along the nice straight road I could see on the map. When I arrived at this stretch, I looked around carefully for a clue as to why but could see nothing. I felt gigglingly guilty as I rode the straight road, waiting for a shout of "HEY, YOU CAN'T DO THAT" but there was nothing. I noted the B&B I would be staying at but with five minutes to riding lesson time, dare not stop. The track to the stable was pitholed and muddy, just as one would expect, so I walked it, not wanting to hit an unseen obstacle underwater and sprawl in the mud after such a successful adventure.

Chapter 3: The Horse

Two ladies awaited me at the entrance. We exchanged hellos. They were the owner and my instructor. "Have you been to your B&B?" they asked. I explained about the missed train and confessed I had not. My lovely hostess had been concerned at my non-appearance and rung the stables to ask if I had arrived. I added an explanation about my technophobic aversion to mobile phones, which caused frowns of bemusement followed by big grins. "I'll ring her and say you will be there at 4.30," the owner offered. "Thank you very much" I replied and was led around to the office with apologies for the need for paperwork. "Its fine," I assured them. "I teach sailing, and we have to do the same." We sorted out a helmet and the required footwear. In Ireland, bicycle helmets are not compulsory, but horse helmets are, which was fine by me as horses are higher, less predictable and more liable to kick if frightened – my bicycle has never kicked out yet. I don't think it's ever been frightened. I have been occasionally dumped by it, however, on its less co-operative days. "Are you alright to ride?" Susan the instructor enquired. "Not too tired?" I laughed. "I'm riding on adrenalin," I said. "Later, I will be tired." She nodded. "You'll sleep well tonight." I wondered if I would. Sometimes, after adrenalin highs I only semi sleep as my brain sorts all the input and wakes me up to discuss any queries it might have. Strangely, it doesn't seem to affect me the next day. We went to meet the horse. Her back was above eye height, and very broad (so if I could get up there, I probably couldn't fall off). I don't do horse colours so in lay terms, she was brown and white with a nice face. We started with me giving her a good brush down while we got acquainted. She relaxed as I got into the groove and leaned gently against the fence. Was she going to sleep? No. This was just a sign of approval. We went to get the saddles and bridles and I managed to not fall over all the trailing bits which tried to slide off as I walked the short distance. I was pleased to be taught how to saddle up, although not sure how much of this went into long term memory after just three days practise. Chevvy was patient and well behaved as I fiddled about with the various bits of metal and leather.

 The first lesson of just five minutes was indoors as I learned stop, start, how to mount, right and left. I laughed internally after mishearing Susan saying turn right. Thinking she said left, I pulled the left rein. Chevvy pulled back to the right, as Susan called out, "No. RIGHT". "OK," I thought. "So I am not really in control. The horse knows what to do and is pretending to do what I say." I found this extremely amusing and also reassuring. If it all went wrong, it wouldn't really be my fault. "That's great." Susan said. "You're riding, Margot." Well, yes I was, and enjoying it, too. We left the riding school. All four of us (Susan, me and a horse each) walked down the muddy track, crossed the wide main road with polite traffic which slowed and stopped to let us cross (Wow) and then remounted for a blissful ride at walking pace through 20ft high sand dunes and along their seaward edge watching the ocean stretching Americawards with the shallow beach wavelets growing into rearing and crashing surf beyond the bay. I leaned forward and whispered in the pricked ears. "I know you know where to go, but I'm just practising," The ears twitched with amusement as I pulled a rein to direct her around a puddle. She was fine with that, she confirmed. The wind was cold through my cagoule. I would wear another layer or two tomorrow, and maybe my gloves which were a last second addition – who wears gloves in March? However, I was happy with that mix of excitement and serenity I always feel when the power of nature surrounds me and added to this was the exhilaration of my first ride on horseback and the achievement of the journey. Could I still go 40 hours with just two hours real sleep? Yes, I could. On the return along the muddy track, Susan's horse splashed through a good sized puddle. I twitched a rein, suggesting to Chevvy that we follow but, establishing her seniority of rank, she hopped up the bank to keep her hooves dry. The puddle ended at a gate. "Oh come on," I laughed. "You'll have to get wet eventually." Susan turned in the saddle. "Bet she doesn't", she chuckled. I was impressed as my bulky mount trotted up to the gate, siddled sideways, sprang her back legs onto the opposite bank and stretched through the gate with a foreleg. She balanced carefully before hopping one back leg back across the puddle and then leapt forward. "She didn't touch the mud", Susan cried with delight as Chevvy walked steadily on. We arrived back at the stables, removed saddles, brushed out the mud, as a way of saying thank you, added rugs and arranged the next day's riding. Internally hopping and skipping and wearing an ecstatic grin I wheeled my bike passed the dodgy puddles and went to find the B&B.

The Guest House was great. A super garage to house my bicycle. An offer of drying facilities. "How did you miss the rain? It was torrential?" That late ferry had saved me a soaking as I would have been cycling over the mountain route when it hit if I had arrived two hours earlier. I offered thanks to the fates. I had even been lucky the cheapest train tickets had gone as my 20 euro ticket was transferable and the 16 euro ticket would have been fit only for the bin. Someone or something was watching out for me and I was extremely grateful.

My room has a shower and I hear the radiators clink as the hot water enters them while I fish around in my rucksack for a towel and the smile keeps coming. What an amazing day. There is one more challenge to come. My technophobe streak extends to electric showers. I am feeling pumped up with success having managed, first time, to switch it on and get the temperature right and then, feeling clean and warm and successful, I can't open the shower cubicle door! It is one of those sliding doors that springs shut to create a good seal and it has no handle on the inside. I can't get my fingers in the groove to push and I can't work out which bit to push to hinge the panels out. I refuse to shout for help. Much too embarrassing. Come on Margot. Work it out. My brain doesn't work well when I get cold. I wonder if I should turn the shower back on while I think but I once saw a film (well the first two minutes of it) where someone is trapped in the shower and scalded to death as the shower gets hotter and hotter and he can't get out so I won't do that, yet, even though I think I could climb over the top of this one if I had no other option. Of course, I know this won't happen here, just focus, Bish. I bend down and get my fingers under the plastic and pull and feel relief as the seal breaks and the door slides back. Margot 1, shower 0. Tomorrow, I will wedge my flannel in the gap. I put it handy so that I won't forget. I try out the kettle and the biscuits and the coffee sachets and relax on the double bed, working out the best side to enjoy the view of the snow covered mountain tops which rise dramatically from the gently sloping plateau within ten miles of where I sit. I edit out the storage unit directly across the road and amuse myself working out that a weeping cherry tree, carefully located would considerably enhance the view without too much pruning needed, but would it withstand the salt laden winds sneaking around the house. Maybe, as those winds have to scale a good sized cliff by the sea before rushing half a mile inland. I get out the map and gloat over my achievement. I'm still a little surprised to be here. Where shall I go tomorrow? My riding lesson is from 10 until 11 so I have half a day to explore. I think, further north, but now it is time to explore on foot and find someplace to eat before an early night.

Bundoran consists pretty much of one long road of shops, pubs, and restaurants, a couple of small housing estates, a closed for the winter fun fair and a cliff top walk well marked with information boards. I find a cosily lit restaurant offering soup and main course, open at 5.30 and enter. It is decorated with yacht steering wheels, lobsters and old style diving suits. I am greeted by a cheerful lady who leads me to a table for two and offers the menu. I'm not an adventurous diner and opt for potato soup followed by lasagne. The soup and roll are perfect. I get quite addicted to potato soup during my holiday – simple, warm and filling. I leave not a drop, scooping the bowl clean with my last piece of bread. The lasagne is also warming in a blow your head off kind of way. Luckily, I tried the sauce first which splashed around the lasagne cliff edge. Gee whiz. Peppers, chili of the hottest kind and possibly curry powder too blended for maximum impact. I seize another bread roll and while chewing, plan my strategy. A mouthful of sauce soaked roll, then one of beef lasagne clear of sauce and this way I will clear the plate but still enjoy the beef lasagne which I do prefer sans sauce. I finish by cooling the gums in lemonade and consider the desserts. In my non adventurous way, I decide to eat a flapjack back in my room, so just have coffee. As I pay, I am asked if I enjoyed my meal. I hesitate. Politeness or honesty? In my business as a gardener, I always ask for honesty because I otherwise can't produce the kind of garden my client enjoys – especially if the garden is overgrown when I first arrive. Do they like the roses 6 metres high or have they just felt unable to prune them? Is the herb Robert a weed or a flower in this particular garden? How about the forget-me-nots? I hope the restauranteurs will be grateful for an honest opinion and tell them. "The soup was perfect. I really loved it. The lasagne in England normally isn't spicy so it was erm a bit of a shock. I liked it but hadn't expected the sauce to be hot and spicy so erm, it took a bit of getting used to," The faces looked a bit sad. "It was nice," I explained "but maybe the menu could say in a spicy sauce". I hope I have not spoiled their evening. Shall I explore a bit more? I have about half an hour's more daylight. I head south and find a small alley of cobbles and quaintness. It leads towards the ocean. None of the shops are open so I meander through and find myself on an undulating cliff path with a sign announcing it to be just 4km long and it is heading in the general direction of the guest house. Perfect. I find signs about fairy holes and a wishing chair and watch the spray fly up from the caves below. I feel sad for the Canadian air crew losing their lives after crossing the Atlantic to fight in the war and hitting the cliff on arrival. I will try the wishing chair sometime, but not tonight because it is getting dark and I still need to find my way back. The white tops of the waves glisten in the decaying light and the sigh and swish of sea becomes more pronounced as sight gives way to hearing. I come to a fenced off common with a huge house in its centre. The building looks sadly derelict and my mind searches for a story to explain its melancholy appearance. Poor house. It's dark now and my body is telling me it's time for bed. I want to be indoors so pick up the pace, once again aware of the chill in the wind. I must have walked 4km by now. I come to a road and try to visualise its landward end. Does this come out by the guest house or was there another turning by the Kentucky Fried Chicken place? I hurry down it. The common on one side with its bleak house and curving cliff on the other. I can see house lights ahead. There's a left turn coming up. I hesitate. I think this takes me to my temporary home, but what if I'm wrong and it takes me too far and then I don't know whether to go left or right at the end. I'm too tired for risks so go straight on and happily arrive at the KFC. Turn left,

Cross one road and the warm glow of the Guest House glints ahead of me. It isn't long before I'm tucked in bed, enjoying the firm mattress, soft pillow and lightweight duvet. I wish my cat, Bubble, a goodnight and send her my love across the ether. Who knows how far cat telepathy extends? Then I descend peacefully into sleep.

I wake the next morning at my habitual time of 5am. Amazing how this happens no matter how short of sleep I am. It is dark outside, not even the mountains glinting. I can hear the wind rushing inland. I make myself a coffee. My hostess has promised breakfast at 8am – half an hour earlier than her welcome pack states. I am grateful. I help myself to a pre-breakfast pack of nuts and study my map – a habit learned from my Dad with whom I used to sit on windy hill tops working out the names of the toy sized villages in the vast landscape spread below us, fascinated by place-names and the amazing forces that carved out our rivers and streams, valleys and plains and created the rising hillsides and steep sided mountains around us. Today, I will ride on horseback and then take my bicycle north, enjoying the coast, and estuary landscape and perhaps a Lough on the way back. I snooze for a while, then stretch out with a bit of yoga – the easy going sort. It's a pleasant surprise to find I am not stiff. What shall I wear to ride in? The snow has blown off the hills and it's cloudy. I think shirt, jumper and anorak and gloves. At 8am I head breakfastwards. There is orange juice and cereal laid out on a side table and a place laid for me. I tuck in. My hostess arrives with coffee and a smile. "Did you sleep well?" I did. She has made me a good hot breakfast and lots of toast. "Where will you go today?" she asks. I tell her my plan. She nods and leaves me to eat and admire the pictures on her walls of boats and flowers, mostly. I have time to take my camera to photograph the sea in its windswept fury before I ride. It's lucky I have done this, because the wind is cold and has a good fierce bite. More layers and a scarf are added to the clothes I wear before I gather my bicycle, snack lunch and drinks. Chevvy is waiting, already brushed

and saddled and keen to get going. Susan
leads her horse out as I arrive. A
corrugated panel to the stable is banging in
the wind. The horses are not worried.
They've seen it before. Susan looks
witheringly at it. "How is it, with builders
that they start a job and then disappear for
days with the job half done?" I grin and
suggest that a lack of payment until the job
is finished often helps. I go and fetch my
helmet and shoes and we are off, back
across the road, which today, is empty and,
after mounting, along the sand dune path.
"I thought we would have a go at trotting
today," Susan says. "Yes please," I say. She
leads us down onto the vast, curving, sandy
beach beneath the acres and acres of sky.
"Stand in the saddle," she instructs. I stand.
"Now bounce as fast as you can." I practise.
She nods. "Hold your reins like so." She
demonstrates and I take a tighter grip. "Off
we go". Chevvy needs no instruction from
me. I find myself bumping around above
the saddle as Susan shouts "Hup,
down,hup,down,hup,down,huo down" very
fast. I find the rhythm although not sure if
the balance is right. Just once I come down

as Chevvy's haunches rise and we give each other a thump. She rolls her eyes back and I sense the disapproval, "Hwhat are you doing oop therrrre?" she seems to ask. "Sorry," I apologise knowing the thump was my fault. She forgives me. Susan pulls up and Chevvy also slows. "That was great," I announce, a little breathlessly but not puffing. We walk a while through the dunes and Susan says she wishes she had brought gloves like me. We chat a little about Ireland, a lot about how lucky we both are to work out in the natural world, the possibility of a united Ireland if Brexit happens. She strongly favours this as a border across Ireland is just nonsensical. I think that England has no rights to Ireland and should not rule from Westminster but think maybe there will be less violence if Northern Ireland has its own parliament for a while – maybe they could work like the USA or Australia with separate states with different laws but one economic whole, I suggest and maybe after a while this would no longer be necessary. Maybe we are both wishing for a dream but I do hope for peace in this dramatic and beautiful land. Chevvy suggests it is time to head home, with a shake of her head at a fork in the path. I think she is bored, I tell Susan who laughs. "Next turn, Chevvy," she promises. We discuss on the way back what we would do if we won the Lotto. Susan would completely revamp the stables to make the horses more comfortable and the teaching area better. I would buy up all the flower rich potential housing land and then not build houses on it, encouraging, instead redevelopment of derelict conurbation land. Neither of us, it transpires will ever carry out our dream as neither of us ever buy tickets for the lotto, but it's nice to dream.

Chevvy lets me guide her back, not the least bit worried about mud on her fetlocks today. "Where will you go, this afternoon?" Susan asks as we unsaddle, brush down and rug up. "Up to the next town and then I'll see", I reply. She advises me to go to the lough but I have a hankering for more sea first. I thank her and the horses and head north. The dirty white clouds are still scudding at high speed across the sky causing the landscape to shimmer in the changing intensity of colours. I'm grateful for the wide cycle lane – also suited to a horse which gives me safe leeway in the side-on gusts, although the traffic is light. I occasionally come across signposts marked with a bicycle but cannot work out what they mean. I hope it doesn't mean "No bicycles" but can't see why this would be the case. Most puzzling. Gradually, small cottages and then terraces of small houses replace the open fields. I come to a wide old bridge across a river, muddy channels with sea birds scuttling from one tasty morsel to another. Steps lead down to the mud, which is about 25 yards across and more steps lead steeply upwards from a quay on the other side. A sign board tells how this was the crossing point for those who had died this side of the river, leading to a church on the hill across the water and well above where I stand. The mourners would sing as the body was rowed across the estuary. Presumably there was no bridge at this time. Isn't Irish history emotional? Such depth. I find it easy to imagine and feel an echo of the sadnesses of times gone by. I remount my wheeled steed and enter the town where I dismount again in order to absorb my surroundings without becoming a traffic hazard. The Irish have done a lot better than the English at maintaining their high streets. All shops are trading and people flit along the pavement and in and out of shops still selling all the requirements of daily life. Is the key, no out of town supermarkets, I wonder, or is it that the Irish still love to socialise? Perhaps the West coast pace of life is still that little bit slower with more emphasis on community and less on rushing home to sit in front of the TV or a computer. I enjoy the atmosphere even under the darkening sky. I explore the winding narrow roads leading to several churches, a tiny harbour and a museum which is sadly closed and gradually become impressed with the many links to famous poets, authors, musicians and artists. It's such a tiny place. I mosey out of town and soon find myself at a mystical site. Locking my bike to a stile, I clamber over it and go to visit a well where people tie rags to the trees as a sort of offering and request and pray to the saint related to that spot. He has a statue set at the back of the wide clear watered well. I spend time on the beach, but find less echo of the past here as the sea gradually laps up the estuary mud and gulls wheel above my head. Perhaps the sorrows flow out with the tide. I am drawn upstream along a narrow path where the water burbles, over pebbles and around boulders, running clear and fast. There is a mill and abbey here, now ruined but undergoing renovation, although nothing is happening today and I have the place to myself. Again the sense of history enwraps me but this time, in serenity. The deepest emotion is peacefulness.

I find it difficult to leave and put a few coins in the collection slot so that others can enjoy where I have stood. Further up the coast, my road dead ends at a beach full of excitement for wading birds but the footpath, which goes across the fields from here is too muddy for trainers so I backtrack to the town and after admiring two more churches and some inlets with stories of the past supplied I find another museum on the top floor of a department store – what a good idea. I find more claims to fame - the author of Frankenstein, and the grandparents of Tony Blair lived here. I wonder if Mr Blair sat in the wishing chair as a child and what he wished for. I now understand the urgency of his government to make peace in Ireland. I am just 2 miles from the border between Eire and Northern Ireland. I imagine the young Tony listening to the heated debates of his elders on dark evenings around a fire. This could easily be where the passion for speech and politics began. There is something about this coastline that allows for clarity of thought and strengthening of resolve. There is a cosy restaurant up here and I tuck into another bowl of potato soup with a roll and butter and then a sumptuous piece of chocolate shortbread. The chat from adjoining tables washes around me. Again, there is that sense of community, of support and everyone knowing one another as people enter and are greeted by name and are asked how their families are faring. Again, my bowl is scooped clean and I head downstairs looking for gifts to take back to England but not really finding anything personal enough.

I have been lucky again. There are puddles outside but the rain clears as I hesitantly open the door, unlock my bicycle padlock and sweep raindrops from the saddle. I glance skywards and offer thanks. Will I try to find the lough? I study a handy wall map and see there are two. One is not so far out of my way and I remember seeing a signpost to it on my way. The other, much bigger, is in the wrong direction and a glance at my watch says I would be then cycling back in the dark. I'll settle for the smaller one. Unfortunately, somewhere I miss my route and then lose my nerve trying to find it again. It is time to go home – well back to my room which now counts as home. I think this road is going the right way but can't remember how it crosses the dual carriageway and where it comes out. Have you noticed how journeys are harder when you are uncertain of the route? It is only two miles, but feels like ten until I cross a bridge over the multilane road below and wind down a narrow lane with an artist's studio on the corner. Oh yes, I remember this from last night's wanderings. Now I am not feeling lost, I decide this is a good time to buy some more batteries. I had had a plan to reduce photo taking by not having masses of spare batteries but this has been hurled into oblivion. There is too much of beauty and interest to be restrained with the camera button, Down one of the town lanes I had come across another harbour with the story of the first people to inhabit Ireland and a drama of mistrust and betrayal between two brothers where one kills the others dog thinking the brother has stolen his wife, but then realises he was wrong and names an island after the dog in repentance. That characteristic of quick Irish temper, and drama inherited from the very first Irish, here, thousands of years ago at the time when Persia ruled the world. How could I not take photographs?

My hostess has seen me arrive and comes to apologise for the weather. I grin. No apology is needed. I am dry, warm and happy and going exploring on foot, but can I check I have the right route for tomorrow as I want to go to Sligo over the mountains and see the waterfall. I just need to check my route out of Bundoran as I have pretty much memorised the rest but didn't know the exact location of the guest house. She calls her husband who is better at this kind of thing. He gives me a main road route but I explain I want to go higher into the hills and down the side of another lough. He promises to look it up on google. I emphasise that it is only the first roundabout I am not sure of and thank them very much. They will leave the directions by my breakfast plate. I go and explore – sitting in the wishing chair and wishing my wish, finding a route down to the beach where we rode and taking my shoes off to paddle. The wind is whipping the sand across the beach in a fine dust but the shallow curve of sand encourages only the tiniest of wavelets to race in with the tide. The beach is vast – miles long and I share it with just one couple and their dog, tiny spots of dancing colour in the long distance. The dog is dancing and leaping with delight, the people less exuberant. My euphoria at this openness rushes in with the wave line and retreats, and soars again. So lucky, I think. At last, I head back, taking pictures of sunlight glittering across the broken water with cliffs descending into the sea beyond. So lucky to have seen and felt all I love to be within. The powerfulness of the sea and open land embrace me, and again, it is hard to leave, even though I feel fulfilled. Can I retain this happiness within me? The spicy restaurant seems too far. I am 55 and have never yet had a KFC. It is time to try one. I have to admit that when I had mentioned a KFC was close to the B&B to Mum she had said "Yuk". I also have to admit that it wasn't to my taste, How can they sell chips made of corn in a land where potato is a staple food and tastes so good? And I do like just a little bit of green stuff on the plate. Millions of people love KFC so I guess my parents just didn't bring me up with a wide enough palate but it was good to eat an apple back at base to wash off the grease from my tongue.

The next day dawned even windier. Another gale was blowing in. Knowing I was horseriding and then cycling 26 miles, my hostess had proudly added baked beans to the already super breakfast and the directions, as promised, were tucked by my plate. In that truly helpful, enthusiastic Irish way, the whole route to Sligo was there. I felt hugely grateful, if a little bit guilty as it wasn't quite the country route I hoped to take, my host sticking to the safer main roads. However, I was now confident of my setting off directions. I polished off the plate, packed my rucksack and saddle bags, checked all drawers, the bathroom and under the bed and pillows for forgotten items, even though I had only unpacked my rucksack for things I'd used while there and then repacked into the rucksack between uses. Who knew where the Irish faery folk would have delightfully hidden things while I was out exploring? After three careful circuits, I was satisfied that nothing was left behind and decided to leave early so that I could walk the wind bedevilled main road to the stables. Once more checking nothing was left behind, I took the key to my hostess and thanked the couple again for a lovely stay. Time to go.

The wind was fierce. When I arrived at the stables there was more chaos than normal. The builders had arrived to fasten back in place the escaping corrugated iron sheets slamming in the gale and using fierce acetylene welding torches in the process. Susan greeted me with a grin. "The horses are upset. We took them around the stables to the other door "*where they are not allowed to go*" to avoid them being upset by the welding and so now they are upset because they are at the wrong end of the stable and went through the door "where they are not allowed to go" to get there" she laughed. " And now we have hailstones, thunder and lightning", she added as there was a crash overhead not made by the builders and their corrugated iron. "We'll have to wait a bit. The horses don't mind being out in the weather but they don't like setting out in it," she explained. My feelings were similar so we gave the horses a brush and allowed them to eat hay while we watched the hailstones bounce around us. I burped and apologised. "It is probably lucky we are delayed," I said. " I was given beans extra this morning to give me extra energy for the journey and I am now feeling the effects." "Oh, right" Susan agreed. We winced as there was an onslaught of thunder and welding torch at the same time. "I remembered my gloves today", Susan announced. "My hands were frozen yesterday". Eventually the storm escaped inland and we headed out of the "wrong door" without too much fuss as the sun sent out a cautionary ray before blazing in full glory around the scampering cauliflower clouds. We walked to the road, and happy now with the routine, I mounted confidently. The horses jingled down the path to the beach. "Are you ready to trot?" Susan asked. "Yes", I said enthusiastically, starting to gather the reins. Susan set off and Chevvy leaped delightedly after her and was most aggrieved when I hauled her back to a walk in slight panic as I still hadn't quite gathered those reins. The eyes rolled back. "What's the problem, then?" she seemed to huff. "Come on slow coach. We're getting left behind". I was ready now. "OK, Go" I said, easing the hold and we were off. The bumpy pace became smooth and I rather suspect I had my first unintended go at cantering as Chevvy closed the gap. We did the movie thing of galloping through the waves and loved it, though still concentrating hard on the right balance and rhythm so I think there is another experience to achieve there one day - the oneness of spirit with your horse. All the same, I had achieved a dream, riding on a rippling waveline, saltwater splashing with the wind blowing in my hair and a happy horse beneath me. Susan slowed ahead of me and Chevvy did the same without my instruction. We walked a different way through the dunes and came to another deserted inlet. Nearly the whole population of Ireland must inhabit Dublin, I thought. Isn't that great for me. On the way back to the stables, Susan's horse gave an almighty exhalation of air from its rear end,

right into Chevvy's nose. Chevvy was disgusted and Susan chuckled. "She must have had some of those beans you were talking about", she laughed.
Chevvy was not amused.

The welders were on tea break when we returned and more riders were on their way so after Susan had kindly taken photos of me with Chevvy, we left the horses in their old familiar place while I went to get changed. I met the new riders looking lost and went to call Susan which saved a game of hide and seek around the stable block and then I was off on the next stage of my adventure, back to Sligo after more sincere thanks for a great experience.

Chapter 4: From Mountains to Lough

The wind was thankfully at my back as I set off east, having carefully checked my route around roundabouts and over bridges and taken the correct right fork in the small village. I hesitated over diverting to look at the lough but I had a long way to go and no guarantee of a good viewpoint on this side of the water. So regretfully gave it a miss, There would be another big lough at Sligo to explore if I wanted. The mountain tops in Ireland are dramatic, rearing vertically from the more gently sloping lower slopes, the brown rock face is cracked and free of vegetation. I will, one day, find a geological map to confirm if this is limestone or some tougher rock. Sheep roam the grassy undulations closer to the narrow road I am navigating. The road indicated by my host is on the other side of the valley and out of sight. I have the mountains to myself and cannot believe the excellent condition of the road under my tyres. The road undulates and, I know, will eventually rise to go over the top of the valley. To my left, and far below I see the end of a smaller lough but it is still a good length. The scenery reminds me of the English Lake District, but without the people. Yes, it is early March, cloudy, windy and only 10 degrees C but still I don't believe the Lakes would have been carless even on this more minor road. I feel exhilarated as I speed downhill in readiness for the next incline. A sheep bounds down the slope on the opposite side of the road to the lough, obviously posing for a photo shot. I used to be slightly addicted to sheep photography, but risk a shot. The sheep baas gratefully and wanders off as I stand and admire the myriad views from this one spot. Then, mount up. Still 22 miles to go. I am ticking off the google points as I go but find a turning at which I am not sure. Is this it? It looks too much like a private track and seems to rise too steeply. I don't want to go up it and then find a dead end. I decide to go on and find myself travelling fast downhill through a small hamlet, not sure if it was on my route or not. Then I arrive at the main road. Bother, it was that turning after all – back uphill and maybe ten minutes away. I always hate backtracking. Should I now go along the main road? I reckon I am now joining my hosts suggested route. I can't get lost as Sligo will be signposted along it, but less good views and more traffic. I sit down and nibble an apple while I study the map, which has only about half the actual turnings marked. Ahead, there appears to be another right turn which would take me back off the main road and then parallel it but what about all those unsignposted, unmapped side turnings. I think I will stick to the main road, and set off, feeling a little let down and annoyed with myself. There's a slight awareness of failure. The right hand turn appears, along with a signpost, not to Sligo, but the named village is on my map so can I, after all find my way back onto my planned journey? I do so want to see those waterfalls. I decide to try it but 50 yards on there's another unmarked junction. Out comes the map and compass. Which road is the one marked on the map? I figure it must be right and pass a church which is on the map. Good. Then there is another three- way choice. One sign points to Sligo but I reckon that goes back to the main road. A car swishes by and then stops ten yards on. A lady gets out. I decide to ask for help as I know my planned route must come in somewhere not marked on the map and I don't want to go down that turning and end up back where I came from. "Hello, I wonder if you can help me", I ask. "Well, I am only visiting my sister", the lady says, "but I will do my best". "I'm looking for the road that takes me to the waterfalls" I explain. "Is this the right one?" "Well, yes," she confirms, "but it's a long way". "Oh that's OK", I reply. "I'm going to Sligo so it's on my way". "Oh well, then yes it's that way and then take the next left to the main road, but if you go the other way", she points back the way I've come, "There are some lovely woods to walk in. It would be a shame to miss them." I pause to think and am slightly amused that she now wants to extend my journey further, even though its already a long way. I thank her but say I don't think I will have enough time and I really do love waterfalls so don't want to miss them. She nods. "Ok. That way then". I set off and encounter yet another junction. Map and compass say left goes to the main road. In fact, it looks like I have to ignore all the left turns and I'll be fine. I FORGOT THE UNMARKED ROAD FROM MY PLANNED ROUTE. At each junction I duly kept right. The road started to rise, with a valley opening to my left, quite steep sided and I could see hills also rising on the far side of the valley. My road began to curve more right which I hadn't expected and rose higher and higher. A new valley appeared with conifers on the hilltops and there was no sign of the lough which marked my waterfall destination. This didn't feel right. The road must bend left again soon. It wiggled a bit. Surely I should be coming to the village I had drawn with its school and church and right turn at the fork. I arrived at the top of a ridge and could see water glinting below me. There it is. I breathed a happy sigh, forgetting all about the village I hadn't seen, but still the road didn't seem quite right. A mini bus pulled up alongside me and a friendly face looked down. "Have you come right over?" he asked. "Isn't it beautiful? Well done." I nodded, and still feeling a little worried asked. "Does this road go to that water? " "Er, yes" he said. "There's a T junction ahead, just go left and then right there." He seemed a little surprised at my intended destination. I thanked him and we both set off. I passed a small cottage with blue sills to the windows and thought that it looked familiar – must be from google I decided but now I'm worried about where the village has gone. The road whirled around several curves and duly deposited me at the lough. The waterfall was marked as halfway along on the far side but I thought I would take a picture from this end where there was a little car park and a slipway. I noticed a board welcoming me to the lake – Must be multilingual, I ruminated as I clicked away. The Irish bit would say Lough not Lake. I went to read the information as there are normally interesting stories about Irish waters and then my heart pumped hard and descended into my socks. "Oh no. I can't have done………I jolly well have…..I've gone in a ten mile circle. This is the lough with the sheep." In fact, gazing uphill, I could see him standing on his favoured rock. How did I do that? I got out the big map and my google map. I'd come back down the road I should have taken first time. My brain went into a useless kind of overdrive as the maps blurred and it took a while for me to regain control and force myself to think sensibly. So how do I get where I have to go? Stupid stupid child. What an idiot. Right round in a circle. Just shut up and be practical. I focussed on my various maps. OK. The good thing is, I now know exactly where I am and which road I have to take over those high moors…..TEN MILES. YOU BANANA!...Just get on with it. I muttered at myself as I pushed my bike back up that very steep hill. WHY DID I FORGET I HAD SAID TO WATCH OUT FOR THE UNMARKED ROAD. WHY HADN'T I CHECKED AGAIN WHEN THE VALLEY DIVIDED? Well yes I know, I was stupid. Get over it. CRIKEY, I'VE GOT TO GO RIGHT BACK OVER THAT MASSIVE GREAT RIDGE NOW. And so the two way split personality conversation continued, raising my adrenalin to deal with the crisis. I felt pretty shaken and was ready to head back to the main road and skip the waterfalls if I got lost just one more time. At this point, it started to rain, which proves an old theory I have that it only rains on miserable people. Well. Eventually I get over that ridge and forcefully tell myself to make sure I go the right way where I went wrong before. I achieve this and at last that evasive village appears. Learning hard lessons, I stop every now and again and check my route and all the little pictures I drew and still get frightened at a junction I didn't draw but remember from the google map sessions. Wasn't I supposed to turn here? My confidence is well and truly knocked. No one to ask. Do what you wrote, but the journey seems hard and not so enjoyable. Why don't the Irish use more signposts? I complain to my inner self. Stop whining, it replies, have more confidence you must be nearly there now. And so I was. The remembered T junction hove into view and a right turn took me around the trees so that the real lough in all its magnificence rippled and wavered ahead of me. "There you are." I cried. "Hooray, I've found you.

You're fantastic", I patted my bicycle. "Well done bike. Well done." My bike accepted the praise quietly and we pedalled on. Here is the car park with signs to the waterfall and I still have time to explore. My legs are a little shaky. I realise I haven't stopped to drink and eat and have a little celebratory lunch while I read the information boards. The lough is huge. These Irish loughs are easily as big as the lakes of the Lake District. I wonder why they aren't as magnetic to tourists, and can only think it is because the Irish take their expansive beauty for granted and don't advertise it. The car park is nearly deserted. The paved path to the waterfall is all mine. I listen delightedly to the burbling brook, a sense of euphoric achievement bubbling, as an echo, within me. I made it. I found the waterfall. I take some photos. Did I do that to capture the beauty or as proof of my achievement? I laugh at myself. Probably a bit of both. I stand and admire the splashing water. I love the power of the falling torrent but also find the continuity, the never endingness somehow comforting. Mankind seems so often to leap up and down on the self- destruct button trying to destroy ourselves, our whole race, but also taking nature with it, and then I look at the eternity of water and hope that when we finally eliminate our own race, the water will continue in its eternal cycle and some of the natural world will rekindle around it. I imagine a world of bright colours as kingfishers flit across streams rushing through forests and meadows filled with dazzling flowers and buzzing bees. If it survives, who cares if I am not here to enjoy it? It is that amazing regularity of noise and movement that eventually replaces euphoria with peace. Time to go. I give the lough a last admiring glance and start my search for the next waterfall. Time is escaping me. I find the footpath but the information board says it is a half hour walk. Regretfully, I search the cliff edge from the road and can see the white splash, like paint, down the crevice but decide not to spoil it by rushing my visit. A photograph will do instead. I had given the next guest house an estimated time of arrival of 5pm and reckon I'm going to be about 15 minutes late if I don't get lost. I concentrate hard, and check my handwritten directions and map often. I've had enough of getting lost. A couple of times I lose confidence in myself. So many roads, all looking the same and not enough landmarks. Once again, going cross country there are no signposts. I come across a marked cycle route with a number, but unfortunately don't know where it goes and hadn't marked it. It ought to go to Sligo as there are no other big towns around here but how much does it meander? My route matches it for a while, which is comforting but then it picks up a main road and heads west. I think it will go to the road I'd headed north on. I am tired now. Should I abandon my map, follow the main roads and start following signposts? I ponder. It seems like failure. No. I still reckon I am on the right route, and my big map suggests if I head south, I can't go very wrong because another main road runs along another massive lough at which I head west. I would have to be about six miles too far east to get this wrong. The road I am on wiggles in all directions chipping away at my resolve and when I arrive at the main road, I am not sure if this is it. It has cars on it, but somehow it doesn't look important. Anyway, I decide to head west. I am now willing a signpost to appear saying Sligo on it, preferably with a small number of kilometres after the name. Come on sign post. I instead spot a landmark from my drawing. Yay. I turn left and mutter the route like a mantra. I am mentally fractured and just want to arrive now. I reckon there is a mental problem which I call "nearly there disease". The last two miles are always the hardest as the adrenalin seeps away. There is a worry ahead because the google map tended to blip as I entered Sligo. One of those bits where cyclists and pedestrians can nip through an alley but the google vehicle could not. Somewhere not far ahead, I would have to ad lib and I didn't have a map of Sligo, only my hand drawn routes out of the station and back to the station from the guest house. At the next junction, I lost my nerve and turned right, even though my route said straight on. Why? I don't know. I knew the right turn would take me to the station and, I think just wanted to be somewhere I knew.

I rationalised by saying I just had to reverse my route from guest house to station, but actually, fatigue was making me irrational. I once read a survival book which stated often, "Do not get tired". Now I knew why. I reached the busy station road and cycled on, passing the station, knowing I had some rights and lefts ahead, complicated by one way systems. Five minutes later, I stopped and tried to work out where I was. I'd gone wrong somewhere. The road I was in looked like the back of the shops, If I went left, I would be back in the town centre and should be able to find a street name on my map. Hooray. This works. Now I am back en route. To be honest, I am fairly furious with myself and my incompetence, but also laughing at the split personality that emerges when the logical side of me snarls at the emotional side. I shrug. That logical bit has had fifty odd years to get used to being over ridden by gut feelings that just get it wrong. I keep hoping that one day I will force the emotional side to submit to logic but only seem to manage this when not tired or when it really, really matters. Anyway, I am on the right main road now and just have to find the guest house. Amusingly, it turns up on what I think of as the wrong side of the road. What is it doing over there? Well, it must be the right one. There won't be two guest houses with the same name on the same road. I cross over carefully, determined not to get run over within sight of my destination. I prop my bike against the porch and try the door. It opens but the inside door is locked. I ring the bell. No reply. I ring again and wait. Still no reply. I try the door knocker, and the bell. Nothing. Well, I'm only fifteen minutes late. They can't have given up on me. I remember they had said I could store my bike around the back in a shed. Perhaps there is a back way in. I have just rung the bell again while I think this so have to wait just another couple of minutes in case someone responds. Nothing. I go round the back and find the shed. Well, bike, you're sorted anyway, I think as I put it away. Now what? No open back doors. I go uncertainly back to the front, and the porch door is ajar. I had shut it. I spring forward and put my finger on the bell. An uncertain face appears around the inside door and I pull the porch door open. "The owner is not here" the face explains. I step forwards wondering if I might need to jam my foot in the gap to stop the door shutting. "I've got a room booked for tonight", I explain. "Can I wait for him inside?" The man opens the door a bit wider but still blocks it with his body. It is starting to rain again in response to my staggering despondent frame of mind. He fishes out a mobile phone and glancing at a card in the window stating "Please ring this number, Michael", rings the number. I assume he is an employee seeking instruction but am surprised that he doesn't know his employer's number or at least have it on speed dial. "There is no reply", he states after listening a while. He glances out at the rain and makes a decision. He steps back and invites me into the hall. I dump my rucksack gratefully. The man opens a door. "You can wait in here", he says. I thank him as I enter what proves to be the breakfast room, but with no breakfast available. He nods and goes off upstairs. I sit on a chair. After a while, I sit on the floor to stretch my stiffening legs. It is a nice room, warm and dry with matching pinewood furniture under white tablecloths and actually there is cereal in Tupperware containers. After 45 minutes, however, I run out of things to admire and start to look for a phone on which to retry the owner – that number in the porch. I find four phones and an alternative number to ring but I can't get any of the phones to work, even the one next to the sign saying ring this number in an emergency. I go back to the breakfast room, having also explored the kitchen where my eyes alight on yet another phone that also does not work. In the hall are some tourist information leaflets and an excellent map of Sligo free for the taking. I lay the map out on the floor and work out all the places I went wrong, wobbling around the town. It turns out if I had simply carried straight on instead of heading for the station I would have crossed a bridge over the river and been immediately on the right road to the guest house. What a Wally I was. I study the other leaflets. There are some nice churches and historical buildings to investigate tomorrow. After that I try lying on the floor for a while. Mmmmm. Not too hard. I could sleep here if necessary. The man thumps down the stairs and pauses in the doorway. "Still not here?" he asks. "No," I reply. He opens the main door and exits. I wonder if I can find an open bedroom. If I can, I will use it. There is an open door opposite. There are beds in here but the bedclothes are disturbed. It might be in use. I don't quite have the nerve to occupy it yet. I can hear some voices upstairs. I have another idea, and even though I'm fairly shy at invading strangers, I decide to knock on all the doors until I find someone with a working mobile phone. The first door I come to is a linen cupboard, so maybe I could invade that downstairs room and make up my own bed. I'll try the phone idea first. The next door is opened by a dark skinned man with limited English, I can see an older lady sitting straight backed in a chair. She is smothered in coloured shawls but looks cold and numb with an emotion which might be despair or shock. I feel like I am invading something private but still ask about a phone. He shakes his head. I apologise for disturbing them and go to the next door. He shakes his head again. "There is no one else here." Under his apologetic gaze, I give up my plan to look for an unmade bed and go back to the breakfast room. The other man returns. "The owner is in Spain", he announces, standing sympathetically in the doorway. "His wife is in Ireland but I do not know her number." I feel a little stunned by such a surprising bit of news but rally quickly. I lead him to the second emergency number and point at the card with both male and female names each followed by a phone number. His eyes light up and he nods again. His fingers dance over his mobile keys and my saviour is soon talking to the wife. "Tell her my name is Margot Bish and I'm booked for two nights", I suggest. When he puts the phone down, he says, "She is coming, Five minutes. You can use this room." He takes me to the room with the rumpled bedclothes. We look at each other and agree that the breakfast room is better just now. It is now passed my bedtime (I am an early sleeper – 8pm is supper in bed time) so I snooze on the floor and clamber upright only when the front door opens giving entry to a somewhat flustered lady in a duffle coat

I scramble to my feet but wait for her to begin the conversation as I am not sure whether to be angry or just plain relieved. Most of all, I just want to lay my head on a pillow and sleep. I think she reads this thought. Without wasting any time, she leads me into the room opposite and looks around. "I'll just get some clean bedding," she says, "Two ladies used this room last night but it'll be fine." I nodded and noted the double bed, rumpled but everything else tidy. I tried to imagine what they were like as my hostess hurried upstairs to get clean sheets. I start removing the old sheets to save time. The lady is back and we replace the duvet cover together, "Sorry," she explains. "We didn't have you written in the book so we closed." There is a pause while she moves round to change the pillow cases. "Did you book online?" she enquires. "Er yes," I confirm. "Ah," she says, "Tis Michael's fault. He does the online bookings but he didn't write you in the book. So now he is in Spain." The logic escapes me here but I don't pursue it. The bed is made. She changes the bin liner and glances up at me. We are both aiming for non-emotional, just exchanging facts but now she needs to gauge my mood. "Are you Ok with this?" she enquires. Luckily, I am. Whilst waiting I had been quietly amused by the situation which seemed so typically Irish, so very laid back and as I snoozed on the floor, I was just relieved I was travelling alone. I couldn't think of a single friend or relative that would have thought this funny and remained calm sorting out the options, and of course, with more people involved there are guilt reactions and apologies and the sense of fault – so whose great idea was this guest house? And if it was mine, then what was I going to do about it? Few of my associates would have agreed we could sleep on the breakfast room floor, just a few would have already taken possession of the bedroom, ready to repel any alternative claimants once the sheets were changed. I shrug. "Mistakes happen and you are doing your best to put it right" I say. " I wonder…." She hesitates, "As we are closed, would you be

OK to make your own breakfast if I show you where everything is, and then the next day we will be open and can do you breakfast then?" She clasps her hands, almost in prayer. I can't think of anything better as my normal breakfast time is 5am – three hours before B&B time. I'd be able to eat and get out exploring much earlier and not waste any day. "Actually, I need to leave early the next day, so shall I make my own breakfast then, too?" I suggest. I had been worried I might have had to forfeit that day's breakfast. I vaguely mention a possible price reduction but I'm not going to push it. Their prices are already low. "Yes. Ok" she says, "I must just ring Michael. He was worrying", Yes, I could imagine he would be, I think. Some people would have been demanding compensation, having histrionics about spoiled holidays and erupting like a volcano. I can do all those things but only when they seem necessary to get a point across. Here, I would be shouting at the wrong person and the effect would have been negative. I am always grateful for the internal voice which analyses, assesses and diminishes emotion. Where had it been earlier in the day when I was cycling in circles? Hah, yes, I know, it was away on holiday – good joke. She is dashing around with duster and dustpan and brush as we talk. Now she deposits them on the stairs. "I'll show you the kitchen." She says. I have a moment's indecision. Do I admit I have already explored it? I decide it is unnecessary information and say nothing. The Syrians are in the kitchen. My hostess has a moment's hesitation of her own and then says hello to them and with a shrug explains that they are just living here for now. She opens the fridge. "Orange juice, or apple. Just help yourself. Help yourself to anything – cheese, butter, bread over there, milk – anything you like. There are cereals in the breakfast room". I have seen them. There is a watermelon in the fridge. I have never tried one. Maybe I might have a small slice tomorrow. The tour is complete. "Are you really OK?" she asks, possibly unable to believe her own luck. I grin. "Sure. It's not your fault" I say. Her phone rings. "That'll be Michael", she says fishing it out of a pocket. As I leave the kitchen, I turn to the Syrians. "Thank you very much," I say. I want to offer more but cannot think of anything I can do to help and no one has actually said they are refugees. I don't want to offend them so I just thank them again more emphatically. What amazing people. So quiet. So helpful when they could have just ignored the ringing bell. I wonder if they are here legally but that is a question that just cannot be asked. I hope life will turn out well for them and feel a surge of anger for our politicians who seem incapable of coming up with an international court system that takes country leaders to court and tries them when they rule in inhuman ways with sentences from never ruling another country to life prison sentences and who knows whether a death sentence is also appropriate. Surely this is more sensible and more of a deterrent than declaring war and blowing up civilians and soldiers alike. Destroying non- combatants' homes and families seems the ultimate way to extend deep emotional hatred of those countries that destroyed their lives. Ultimately, the blame lies with all our political leaders and the makers of arms – not just nuclear but anything more lethal than a single bullet gun. These makers of death will create war zones for as long as they are allowed in the interest of profit. Personally, I don't know how they can live with themselves.

I am ready for bed but first must psyche myself up to deal with yet another new shower or I will be too stiff to explore tomorrow. I unpack pyjamas, soap and towel (just in case they are missing from the bathroom). The bathroom window is rattling and occasionally whistling and moaning in the rising wind. Another gale has just discovered Ireland. Wisps of cold air ooze around the badly fitting frame. Luckily, the radiator is hot and the shower cubicle has a wide screen eliminating draughts – I will be warm in the shower if the water is warm and I have my night clothes within reach to don before being exposed to that cold air. I am getting good at this shower thing – right temperature first time and a good water pressure too. There is shower gel and a clean towel. All is well. The bed feels vast but comfortable. I

make and drink a soup and eat some nuts
while I plan tomorrow's adventure.
Something where I can't get lost, I think.
Like all round the lough. I measure it. About
ten miles, and then time to explore Sligo.
Maybe I might also go find a beach but (I
smile happily) I have already been on some
fantastic beaches so this is not essential.
Route planned, stomach filled, I switch off
the light and have just ten seconds to
assess traffic noise before falling asleep.

I wake at six – wow – I have kind of
overslept. I start with a coffee in bed while I
think about clothes and food to take out
today. I need to save some rations for
tomorrow which will be a long day
travelling and not many places to buy food
until I'm on board the ferry. My brain
stutters here as I remember the ferry non-
breakfast. Surely there will be an evening
meal on board. Anyway, there is a town at
the other end of the lough so I can get
something there today for lunch, and a
snack in Sligo for my tea tonight. Time to
get some breakfast. I laugh at myself

tiptoeing to the kitchen, carrying a glass and dish with cereal already poured into it. I haven't been able to work out the efficient way - jugs of milk and fruit juice to the breakfast room or glass and dish to the kitchen? I think I have got it right as I pour and drink an orange juice and then refill the glass with a mixed fruit juice – very tasty. Milk on cereal. I find some spread and some fresh rolls and cheese. Toast? There is an industrial sized toaster which I reckon needs an apprenticeship to operate so settle for cold croissants instead. The slice of watermelon balances neatly in the cereal bowl with rolls and croissants balanced on top. I had spotted a kettle, water urn and hot chocolate powder in the breakfast room the night before, so I reckon I am sorted as I pad back to the breakfast room. It is quite a long walk. I suspect that toast is rarely hot by the time it has travelled the distance. I feel only slightly deprived of eggs, bacon and sausages. Another hot chocolate and a bite of croissant make me philosophical about this. There is nothing to keep me. I consider the etiquette of clearing the dishes when you've paid for breakfast and then been asked to make your own. If I go half way and leave things in the kitchen, the Syrians might feel they have to do it, but washing up when not offered a reduction is not on so I leave everything used neatly stacked in my place. It is still gale swept outside and the clouds race across the sky in ragged lumps of grey, black and white as I open the shed door and greet my bicycle. Rain is possible. I pack cagoule and waterproof trousers but wear just an anorak and tracksuit trousers. Map, nuts and apples are packed, as is my camera. I am getting the hang of the town now and set out walking along the river but disciplining myself about diverting to explore. Lough first and then the town.

There are swarms of children neatly uniformed walking to school. They are all well behaved and I am excited to see no cars dropping children off. The youngsters walk in groups and chat with animation. There are almost no adults in attendance. I wish this was still the way in England. The children seem happier in their independence and it reminds me of the 2 mile walk to school I used to do with my friends in Chester during which we would discuss homework, the teachers, other classmates and our developing views on the world. It was the cement of a long lasting friendship. It also benefitted our education. We were a mixed group. Some of us good at maths and science, some at the arts and some at English so where one of us was struggling, the others could help. In a class of 30, the teachers taught and we listened and rarely got any personal tuition. How sad that today's English children cannot share their knowledge and gain confidence in this way. Such are my thoughts as I leave the town behind. The nearest end of the lough is further away than I thought. I stop a couple of times to check I'm going the right way. I see there is a wood before the water, with footpaths marked. This would make up for missing the suggested wood walk yesterday and give me a break from what is proving to be a busy main road. The weather is not great. Grey skies and a touch of drizzle. The trees might give some shelter (I hope). This road is much more peaceful, just one car in two miles. I get a glimpse of the lough and then I am in amongst the trees and arrive at a car park with a well detailed map. Should I leave or take my bike. Easier to leave it but there is stuff in the saddle bags and I note that I might miss this car park on the way out. I hope no one will mind the tyre tracks. I won't be riding. The path is mostly all mine. I meet a couple of colourfully waterproofed ladies and one dog walker with a smiley dog of mixed parentage. And probably mixed grandparentage, too. My plan has worked. The lough stretches mistily into the distance, pockmarked with raindrops but the fresh green leaves above my head break up the wetness into a fine spray blown on the wind. Every now and again I come across a numbered board entertainingly written. Some tell of the history of the islets I can see, others identify the trees and even explain how to recognise them elsewhere. I play trying to identify before reading and feel chuffed to only get two wrong. There are rowing boats moored occasionally. I would have loved to borrow one and row on this amazing stretch of water surrounded by woods and hills but they are mostly padlocked and oarless and there is no one to ask. I stop in a small bay with a patch of sand and eat an apple. I feel lucky. Lucky to have had the free time and money to make this trip, to have the level of fitness required to explore and have adventures. Lucky to have had a dad who taught us to ride bicycles and explore. Lucky to have a mum who allowed us our independence and trusted us to stay safe so that exploration at peace with myself, truly in touch with my surroundings is something I am not afraid to do. So many miss out on things they would love to do because they are afraid to go alone but I find it is easier to make new friends and chat to locals if I am not in an insulated group. The wood is old, but not natural. I find a sign telling me the land all at this end of this lake was bought in the 1800's and the owners purchased and planted hundreds of trees at an enormous cost – it still seems enormous in today's money. I am grateful to them for this beautiful place but also gulping that at that time of potato famine and poverty, someone had money to throw away on so many trees and then donate the wood to the people. My feelings are well and truly mixed, especially as I reflect that the money probably came from slavery or workers employed in horrendous working conditions. The world is a very complicated place. I put the historical conundrum aside and concentrate on the next board which tells me a hermit lived on one of the islets I am now looking at and the next islet has unusual grasses planted especially for wildlife. I look at my watch. Better shift on a bit. I've still got a lot of miles to cover. Eventually I find my way back to the main road, having established there are no short cuts to be had. The rain is still falling so I hop around putting on waterproof trousers and add my cagoule and cap – hoods always fall over my eyes unless I add a cap under the hood and end up with a profile like a duck. Why do they put so much material into the hoods? I can see the lough now, still misty but then this looks more romantic and dramatic and so far it is not the really wet kind of rain. I notice I am on a cycle route with kilometre markings, but as they decrease, I realise, I don't know where they are counting down to. Is it back to Sligo? It's more than the distance to the town at the other end of the lough. Anyway, it makes me feel good as the kilometres click by. I come to a small castle with a car park and a slipway. I'd like to look around it but it is all locked up. There is a ferry moored up with a notice. I wonder if I could skip the cycle ride and take a ferry right back down the lake. What a wonderfully lazy way to travel. I feel that so far I have exercised plenty and spent little. The idea is extremely tempting. When does the ferry go? In typical Irish fashion, there is no one to ask. A sign advises the ferry will go at 2pm, but only if there are at least 10 passengers. It is now midday. If I wait until two and then it is cancelled, I will still have to cycle and I am now about half way round. I gaze around at the people free scenery and wonder how much I would have to pay to get the ferry to go with just me on board. Too much, I decide. Nice idea but not going to happen. The dangling of that temptation makes it hard to remount and cycle into the now heavy rain. Not torrential but I am aware of clinging waterproofs and the need to squint. Where's that town? I am ready for hot food and some shelter. The next sign is at a junction and tells me the town is close – hooray. There are a few old buildings to gaze at, but more importantly, a small supermarket selling hot pasties amongst other things. Perfect. I find a characterful bus shelter to sit in while I eat and watch as the rain gradually eases. There is a map outside the supermarket explaining the cycle routes. There are several, with most routes about 20km. It looks as though I will be pretty much following one back to Sligo – good. I am close to the "lake isle of Innisfree". A poem I loved at the age of 14. I used to dream my English lessons away, imagining I was there and not studying H.E Bates at the top of our tower block school. The isle pretty much lives up to expectations, although I had thought it was in Scotland until this day when I find it in Ireland. The map had kindly warned me about all the steep hills on the way back and also several "must see" viewpoints along the way. I think it's great I have no deadlines today and can explore to my heart's content. What a fantastic sense of freedom. Can't help whooping as I whizz down the next hill. The rain has stopped. The wind has eased. The next viewpoint appears right on time. This one requires a scramble uphill through woodland flowers, tall trees and over ascending boulders and the lough spreads, rippling, well below my feet. My camera has evolved its own system of dramatizing my photos by only partially opening the lens cover. I have to admit it looks good, but how frustrating it is that I need a battery to remove a lens cover. I am more than capable of doing this with my fingers, and can even do it quicker. I much prefer my childhood cameras which didn't take precious seconds digitally focusing while the light changes or the subject of the picture flies away. They had no need of a battery except to add flash, which I could choose to add so that I controlled the light settings. It drives me into a severe muttering fit when my too smart camera corrects the light levels. Why can't it just take the picture in front of it? I once had a camera that auto focussed but left everything else to me, and having only

36 exposures made me careful with what I clicked at. I love to browse my old photos but find it fiddly running through computer files or camera memory discs to find what I want to look at. There's the technophobe trait showing again! Anyway, I forgive my camera its complexities just this once but hope I can work out a way to eventually fix it. The lough is moody and impressive. I wonder again why the Irish don't promote this gift more. There are also rippling brooks at the bottom of the hill. I stop to watch the swirls and eddies as I nibble a flapjack and then move on, reminding myself I still have Sligo to explore.

It takes another hour to get back. I go back to my room and drink a soup, stretch my back and legs and then head back into the town, I have a knack for finding museums to explore on the day they are closed. Today, I excel at this, finding three, but in between these disappointments, which I can't help laughing at, I find a beautiful stretch of river, a tiny art gallery shared and jointly run by four students from the local art college. I admire their art, their enthusiasm and courage in setting up their own shop. I wish them well and buy some birthday cards to help them on their way. The town is busy. Narrow pavements are filled with people and a few too many cars are rattling along the roads. There is a measure of tolerance between drivers and pedestrians, both acknowledging the difficulties of finding space on the pavement and allowing a flow of traffic. I do my best to not hold anyone up as I peer into windows looking for gifts, postcards and something to eat. A small precinct proves the ideal solution. No more cars to dodge and here is a popular self-service restaurant serving my now favourite potato soup and a roll and some delicious cookies, too. Once fortified I quickly find a bookshop selling postcards and a book of Irish sayings, and a gift shop to add further presents and then, in a surge of sentimentality buy three more postcards from a hopelessly disorganised and dusty back alley shop where copper saucepans are stacked on top of Irish flags and pottery leprechauns and there is barely room to move. The man in charge is the first Irish person I have met who doesn't smile. I wonder if he is recently bereaved. Back in the street, I consider what to do next. Have I time and energy to recross the river and go to find a last beach on which to walk or should I just cycle to the estuary on the town side. It seems to have been a long day. I have seen so much and I don't want to spoil it by getting too tired so I pedal into the strengthening wind through a sort of retail industrial area with the river widening to my right. In places I can see seabirds sifting the mud. I try to work out if the tide is rising or falling. I think this must be nearly low tide from the dribble of water in the deep channel. I reach a dead end but I can glimpse the ocean and a couple of navigation marks. There is that smell of salt and far away places on the wind over the underlying scent of mud. The wind is cold now I am not burning energy pushing into the wind. It is time to go back to my room and draw pictures of my memories. It will be a giggle this holiday as I really am hopeless when it comes to drawing horses, but it is almost a tradition now, having done this for about my ten last adventures. Sometimes it is impossible to capture the essence with a camera (digital or not).

I can hear that there are more people around when I open the guest house door. There are voices murmuring above my head and the occasional thud of feet on the ceiling, but no one is in sight and I can't think of an actual reason to track down my host. It may even be less embarrassing if we don't meet so I go to my room, kick off my shoes, switch on the kettle and am soon engrossed in my picture diary. I can hear the odd thump and bang from other rooms but reckon I am tired enough to sleep through anything when I am ready to bed down. I have another shower, eat all the food I won't want tomorrow and am soon fast asleep.

The next morning, I again wake early. Quarter to six, my watch says. I snooze a bit but feel quite thirsty. I could really do with an orange juice. I consider the ethics of getting up an hour earlier than I intended and fetching a glass of juice from the kitchen. I'm not stealing because I would have drunk the juice later anyway so there is no reason for the itch of guilt as I creep kitchenwards armed with the glass from the bathroom. No one is in the kitchen. I open the fridge and find the milk and juice jugs are gone. Ah ha. They must now be in the breakfast room because the guest house is now officially open and breakfast is set up for the guests. I take my glass to the breakfast room and this is where I encounter a bit of a snag. How could I possibly guess that the movement into the room, or possibly the opening of the door would cause the radio to burst into life? I wince and internally groan. Remembering the movement noise I experienced last night, I reckon the room above my head must be able to hear the radio and it's still only 6 o' clock, What to do? Perhaps the radio is movement sensitive and if I quickly get my juice and leave it will stop. I hurriedly fill my glass and carefully shut the door behind me, nipping back into my room across the hall. I climb back into bed and sip my drink but on finishing and lying back down, I can still hear the radio. I nearly get back up to go and turn the sound down, but then think the radio might be on a timer and if I go back, I will start a new cycle, so I lie and send mental indian smoke signals of apology to anyone I have woken early. I think the other guests might think it is their hosts working in the kitchen but have no way of telling them that I am the guilty perpetrator as I will be gone before they arise.

I work out what time I must leave and then work backwards, time to eat, time to dress, time to pack. So, get up at seven. I reset my watch alarm but in fact am so awake by 6.45 that I get up, have a coffee and dress, then pack and just keep going. The radio is now playing Irish folk music. How did it do that? Clever. I munch cereal, and croissants and enjoy another hot chocolate which reminds me of a field trip to France where every breakfast consisted of croissants and hot chocolate and every evening meal had red wine. After 8 days of this I couldn't wait to get back to England and what I think of

as "Proper food". Ironically, the day I
returned was my birthday and Mum had
specially bought red wine to celebrate with
our lunch. Thankfully, there were no
croissants. Anyway, that was many years
ago and I do now enjoy the occasional
croissant. I did make a point of drinking the
hot chocolate alongside my bowl of muesli,
however.

I successfully cycled straight to the station.
Not one single erroneous detour and so
arrived twenty minutes early. I read all the
leaflets and was relieved to find I had
visited every possible attraction that was
open and then read all the other notices
several times before trying out the toilets –
beautifully clean and tidy. Irish railways are
really something to be proud of. The only
railway I have tried which was comparable
was in Portugal. Another country with a
history of poverty but with beautifully
made up roads and a fast, punctual,
comfortable railway system. I hope that
one day, England and Wales might catch
up, but then again, the piecemeal setup of
about twenty different companies annually

tendering for contracts to run tiny sections of track really doesn't encourage investment and efficient development. Still, at this moment in time, I am admiring the gleaming, almost soundless coaches streaming up to the buffers on platform 1 twenty minutes before departure. I climb happily on board, place my bike in the bike rack and relax into a seat, soft, wide and clean. Even the windows are gleaming.

Chapter 5: And Home Again

I spend the journey back alternately admiring the scenery, looking at my map and listening carefully to the Gaelic announcements. Surely, after twelve announcements, identical except for the name of the station we are approaching and which I can see on the map, I ought to be able to say, in Gaelic, "We are now approaching……. Please mind the gap when leaving the train. Thankyou for travelling with Irish Rail." The only thing I actually achieved was rail which sounds like iron road. How lovely I thought what a good description. I then realised that actually rail way is pretty similar.

The train arrived in Dublin exactly on time. I had about three hours until the ferry left so thoroughly enjoyed pushing my bicycle along the riverside walk in bright sunshine and being impressed again at the spaciousness and combination of new black glass with old brick. There was none of the jarring and jangling that the London skyline creates in my head with way too many different shapes and higgledy piggledy heights and building materials. We really seemed to have lost the art of architectural harmony. The Scots still have it. The Irish have it. The Canadians have it. The English had it right up until Victorian times but somewhere it is now buried under the rubble. I managed to stay on the right side of the river and navigated the route around the tunnel into the docks and dawdled up to the ferry terminal where I was greeted by two cheerful chaps ready to book me in. They explained what to do with my bicycle and gave me a label to attach to it so that it couldn't get lost and I headed in prepared to sit on the floor if the seats were of the same uncomfortable plastic as Holyhead. How lovely. There was an open snack bar serving coffee and cake at very decent prices so I use up a lot of my change and the material covered seats are perfect to collapse into with sunny views of the lorries being loaded. The queue seemed endless. It sure brought home the amount of trade taking place between Ireland and England.

Wow, the whole of England will need to be employed as customs officials come Brexit, I thought and ferry bookings will require lorries to turn up twenty hours before loading. It was hard to get my head around the concept. Maybe, they just won't bother, I thought. As in many things, people may disregard the rules in the interests of common sense. Two nice people entered from a door linking to the car loading area and politely asked to see my passport and boarding pass. Were they practising for Brexit? They were happy with the bits of paper and went to get themselves coffees. More people filtered in but it is amazing how few foot passengers travel by ferry. There was a form available to comment on how much you enjoyed the journey so I amused myself squeezing my thoughts concerning the barren and bleak facilities of Holyhead into spaces too small for my constructive criticism. Dublin, I said was pretty much perfect apart from a lack of maps on how to get from the ferry port to the stations and perhaps these could even be put on the walls of the ferries.

Once again, I am lucky with the weather. Yesterday's gale is abating and the wind is still from the west. We will arrive early. The ferry layout is different. I am disappointed not to be able to watch the untying of mooring lines but console myself with a huge plate of lasagne which I am allowed to pay for with a mix of euro coins and English pounds which will save me trying to pay for stuff in Lidl's with euros when I get home. There is a "quiet room" which nearly lives up to its name and I sleep for a while. There is an interlude of excitement when two children, replete in Irish costume dress – must be either a dance competition or a wedding, I surmise- and too young to read notices burst in and have a rough and tumble wrestling matchin the middle of the floor before a serious and smartly suited older Irish lad firmly removes them from the area. I had been quite enjoying the entertainment. It is turning dusky as we leave Ireland behind and I enjoy watching the ferry dance between the navigation lights of the winding channel out of the bay.

I use my compass to check the course we are steering and reckon we are crossing a north-moving tide. After a while, I start to write the tale of my adventure, which is more or less what you are reading now, but arrival at Holyhead means a postponement of completion. I watch the landing with awe and admiration. The manoeuvring space is small and the slipway has some pretty exact markings to land on. Is it a manual or computerised system I wonder? Anyway, it works perfectly and I am impressed (having botched very many landings of my 12ft sailing dinghy in the past) as we hit target first time. I am relaxed now about our departure from the ferry. I have a good margin to train leaving time, and know the station is actually part of the ferry port. No chance of getting lost again. We are allowed to sit on deck F until the ferry is docked and the priority lorries have landed and then we clatter down the stairs to the bus which gives us a night time guided tour of the port – very pretty with all those lights. I am soon reunited with my bike which has only lost one light and I have a spare so that's OK. I am fascinated by the energy levels of a four year old on her second wind. The family of Mum, teenager and said four year old are all dressed in pyjamas and dressing gowns. Mum looks exhausted and I consider if the four year old is somehow dredging energy out of her mother. I am delighted with her ballet dancing performance – most graceful and only slightly alarmed by her gymnastics beam exercises along the arms of the seats. Mum is not concerned so this must be normal behaviour. The train is on time but it is now about 8pm and the journey ahead is still long. I pause to count the stations we will stop at. A man in uniform asks if I need help. "I'm just seeing which stations we stop at," I explain. "All of them", he says dolefully and goes on his way. I find the bike hooks and my seat, The Irish family are opposite, the youngster still hyperactive, mother still tired and the older sister trying to calm her sibling with wrathful utterings of gaelic which end in tears as the youngster is blocked into her seat. Mum is unsympathetic. They all fall asleep as the train shudders along the North Wales coast. Mum wakes with a start and asks if this is

Chester. "About four stops to go", I tell her. The girl has also woken and somehow wriggles past her sleeping sister as her mum dozes off again. The ticket collector walks down the train and I am impressed as the four year old politely asks where the toilet is in English and takes herself off there before returning and snuggling back up in her dressing gown. She is singing and dancing again by Wrexham and although I like her bounce and style I look forward to some peace when they leave at the next station. As we arrive in Chester they gather their things and I feel an echo of the excitement I used to feel when revisiting my old home but this time I am not disembarking.

That internal voice is laughing at me as the Irish family are replaced by four Welsh adults who have been celebrating a Welsh rugby victory, The ladies in particular are somewhat overjolly and inebriated and sing Welsh songs in a surprisingly inharmonious duet. Is it only the men who have melodious timbre? So much for a bit of peace and quiet. The top tune seems to be

Delilah which becomes a little tedious after five or six renderings. To compensate, some English lads further down the train launch into Swing Low Sweet Chariot and the competition gradually hots up. Caught in the middle, an elderly lady removes herself to another carriage. I wonder at which station the singers will leave. Birmingham is the last stop and still about ten stations away. The train route does considerable wriggling to and fro across the Anglo Welsh border. I do not see or hear what happens to escalate things but suddenly, the Welsh ladies are upset and hurling personal remarks down the train. One of them calls out, "I hope you have Nationwide Bank Accounts because I work there and next time you come in I will refuse to serve you." I conclude from this that when not drunk she is intelligent and polite and a good worker but the alcohol is certainly clouding her judgement. I do not hear the English response but then the Welsh advance down the train saying it was all a bit of fun, but body language somehow more threatening. I am bewildered by the mounting aggression. Up until now, the Welsh blokes

have remained uninvolved, but suddenly
the guy in front of me says, "Right. That's
enough. I'm going to smash their faces in."
Oh cripes. I think. If they start a fight, the
train will be delayed and it will be midnight
before I reach Birmingham. In desperation,
I reach forward and grab his jacketed
elbow, pulling backwards and downwards.
This seems to have the desired effect of
anchoring him to his seat. "Look," I begin. "
I'm neutral in this, but please don't fight.
I'm going to Birmingham and even now it
doesn't get there until half eleven. Please
don't make it later." I glance diagonally
across the aisle and see his friend is staring
at me incredulously. I mouth across to him
"Stop him" and after the tiniest hesitation
he turns to his mate and says. "They're not
worth it. Just a load of silly English idiots
who haven't the brains to have manners". I
feel the arm in front tense more and then
relax. "If you let me go," he says, "I'll go
into the next carriage and calm down", I let
go slowly and he is as good as his word. The
Welsh ladies are still up in arms, marching
about the carriage but I now have the other
bloke calling them back, saying to leave it.

One lady comes back and tries to get him to support them, but I have had enough and now stand up to block her from going back to the fray and say "Please, calm down, Its gone far enough." I try to remain calm and firm and hold her eye but also don't move out of her way. "I want to get my daughter", she says. Now I'm really surprised. She has not behaved in a good example way. I just could not ever imagine my mum acting that way and especially not with me or my sister present. My jaw does that dropping in amazement thing but I pull myself together and say, "Just call her. There's already too many people down there". Gradually things ease and I am trembling but relieved. As we approach Godowen, there is a last bit of aggressiveness as the Welsh suggest the English get off the train here, with the Welsh to have a fight which the English "are sure to lose" The English lads protest that as they live in Shrewsbury they don't want to get off here. "Cowards". The Welsh cry as they leave the train. I am still shocked by the alcohol induced aggression. This wasn't yob or gang culture but people in middle class jobs, dressed tidily totally unable to act with common sense due to a drink or two too many. The remaining English, let off steam and groomed rumpled feathers in retelling the event as a dark comedy. I think they were also shocked by the aggression they had unleashed in what had started as a joke. Two guys come into our carriage and take the vacant seats. I look at them apprehensively. Will there be another drama? They chat between themselves and seem unaware of the slow draining tensions. Much to my amazement, as we pull into Shrewsbury, the Welsh are there, coming up the platform stairs with two police officers. How did they travel so fast? I hope the lads won't get into trouble because I feel they were not the aggressors but there is no way I can give my name to anyone as a witness without getting off the train which would mean not getting home at all this night. I feel the story is so amazing that I point out the two groups to the strangers in the seat opposite and relate the story as the train leaves them all behind. My listeners seem suitably impressed by my tale. They leave the train at the next station and I am left now in a peaceful carriage. The ticket collector comes to check my ticket and I tell him there was nearly a fight, I explain what I saw in case the police ask him about it. He nods glumly. "Last week we had two sets of football supporters on here and the police. The supporters started fighting and then when the police arrested them, they fought the police and we stopped at a station and the doors opened and the police fell out with some of the supporters and called to us to carry on so we did but there were still some supporters on the train and they kept fighting so I left them to it." He pauses. "I don't think I'll be staying in this job much longer." I can't blame him. We pull up in Birmingham on time. All I have to do now is cycle 15 miles home in a storm of freezing rain and hailstones. As I exit the station, I hear an announcement "The Redditch train is arriving at platform….~ I pause. Theoretically, the Redditch train should have departed fifteen minutes ago. Can I catch it? Maybe I should have tried but I am psyched to cycle and at the wrong end of the station. Too annoying if I sprint all that way and arrive as the train departs. I pull up my hood and accidentally leave by the wrong exit. Birmingham at midnight is an alarming place. Even in the hailstorm, there are revellers boogying in the street to some unheard beat, glass of alcohol in hand. No one looks aggressive but my recent experience has fuelled my wariness. I have a theory that the baddies of the world are more likely to pick out people who don't look confident about where they are and where they are going. With this in mind, I pushed off confidently in the general direction of away from the station. Once out of the way, I would find some road signs and work out where I have confidently cycled to. The plan begins well. No one confronts me and gazing surreptitiously around for interest, and not finding any, I sidle up to a street map of the sort that says "You are here". Then curse myself. I have been cycling north when I should have been heading south. I have never yet cycled the right way out of Birmingham New Street but this is the most impressive bungle yet. I start to work out how to correct without backtracking –

someone might notice and out of the corner of my eye become aware of a face close to mine. It is not a horrible face and could have been quite nice in other circumstances but in the streetlights it is white to the point of bloodlessness and wears a look of extreme worry just inches from my nose. I wonder what he thinks he is looking at and what he has been taking. To be on the safe side, I take a small step backwards whilst assuring him in an attempt at a calm voice that everything is OK, everything is fine, and in my head, add just don't do anything to change this. I take a second larger step back. Attempt a reassuring smile and scarper, heart beating at a surprisingly rapid rate. So pale! I cycle on and eventually reach some proper roads with signs but the route I want is closed and I am forced to cycle through the tunnels which reminds me of another horror movie I watched five minutes of where the cyclist doesn't survive the tunnel. Fortunately, I emerge unscathed and wonder if I have just broken any laws. Somehow, I navigate a sort of inner ring road and just after I think I have lost the route to the A441 and will have to go down the A38 and cut across, I find I am already on the A441. How did that happen? I mean good but well wow, Magic. The rest of the story is humdrum. I do the normal mutterings about non dipped headlights and inadequate lighting on the Alvechurch road and arrive home only 35 minutes later than expected to a rapturous welcome from Bubble the cat who urges me to get us both fed, supervises the filling of the hot water bottle, the finding of pyjamas and the leaping into bed. There is very little better than being greeted by a cat who has badly missed sleeping against my warm body for seven nights and is now purring a contented lullaby as she plumps up her human cushion, circles twice to create the right contours and then purrs me to sleep, greatly content to be home, safe, warm and dry. There is nothing like an adventure filled holiday to remind one of the important things in life and how lucky I am to have them. Food, shelter, drink, a warm bed and the love of a cat.

Printed in Great Britain
by Amazon